CUYAHOGA VALLEY

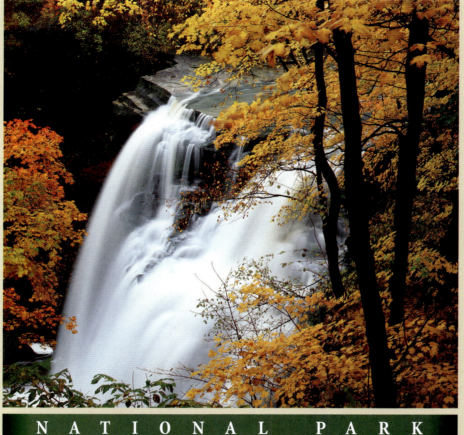

NATIONAL PARK

A PHOTOGRAPHIC PORTRAIT

IAN ADAMS AND JIM ROETZEL

Copyright © 2005 by
Twin Lights Publishers, Inc.

All rights reserved. No part of this book may be reproduced in any form without written permission of the copyright owners. All images in this book have been reproduced with the knowledge and prior consent of the artists concerned and no responsibility is accepted by producer, publisher, or printer for any infringement of copyright or otherwise, arising from the contents of this publication. Every effort has been made to ensure that credits accurately comply with information supplied.

First published in the United States of America by:

Twin Lights Publishers, Inc.
10 Hale Street
Rockport, Massachusetts 01966
Telephone: (978) 546-7398
http://www.twinlightspub.com

ISBN-13: 978-1-885435-59-2
ISBN-10: 1-885435-59-2

10 9 8 7 6 5 4 3 2 1

(right)
Red maple leaves cover the rocks below Blue Hen Falls in Cuyahoga Valley National Park near the village of Boston Mills. A half-mile downstream is another cascade, Buttermilk Falls.

Book design by
SYP Design & Production, Inc.
http://www.sypdesign.com

Printed in China

Dedication

*This book is dedicated
to the memory of
Linda Wieditz*

Introduction

American Indians called it "Ka-ih-ohg-ha"—crooked. The 95-mile Cuyahoga River rises in the glaciated wetlands and farmlands of Geauga County in northeast Ohio and flows south to Kent before turning west to Cuyahoga Falls, tumbling over waterfalls and rapids through Gorge Metropark before turning north and entering the Cuyahoga Valley. For the next 22 miles the river meanders through a broad valley hemmed in by forested hills east and west…the Cuyahoga Valley National Park. At Valley View the river leaves the park, glides under Interstates 77 and 480, and winds through Cleveland's industrial Flats before emptying into Lake Erie, a scant 30 miles from its source in Geauga County.

The Cuyahoga Valley offers nature lovers a plethora of spring and summer wildflowers as well as dramatic fall color. In recent decades beaver have returned to the valley, together with wild turkey, eastern coyote, and a burgeoning population of white-tailed deer. More than 200 species of birds have been observed in the national park, and 130 species are regularly tallied by enthusiastic birders during the annual spring bird count. A recently launched Countryside Initiative seeks to restore the rural character of the area by promoting small-scale farming efforts in parts of the Cuyahoga Valley.

Hikers and cyclists can travel the 20-mile Towpath Trail along the banks of the old Ohio and Erie Canal, and a section of the 1200-mile Buckeye Trail passes through the national park. History buffs are welcomed at Hale Farm and Village, a recreation of an 1840s Ohio Western Reserve farming community. Visitors who prefer a more relaxed pace can board the Cuyahoga Valley Scenic Railroad, which offers rides from downtown Akron to Independence. Music lovers gather in summer at Blossom Music Center, on the eastern edge of the Cuyahoga Valley, which offers popular music concerts and is the summer home of the world renowned Cleveland Orchestra. Skiers visit the slopes at Brandywine and Boston Mills Resorts when the snow flies.

The authors have been exploring the Cuyahoga Valley through the lens for more than a quarter of a century, and offer this book as a celebration of the natural and historical wonders of this precious green space between Akron and Cleveland. For those who know the area well, we hope the book will evoke memories of pleasant times spent in the Cuyahoga Valley, and perhaps reveal a few new ones as well. For those who have not visited the national park, we hope that the book will open their eyes to the beauty, history, solitude and recreational opportunities offered by this northeast Ohio treasure.

The authors would like to thank the staff of Cuyahoga Valley National Park, especially John Debo and Jennie Vasarhelyi, and the staff of The Cleveland Metroparks, for their encouragement and support. Margaret Tramontine and Lynn Huber of Hale Farm and Village were most helpful during our photography visits. Finally, we would like to thank Paul Sylva and Jean Patey of Twin Lights Publishers for commissioning the book and making it a reality.

—Ian Adams and Jim Roetzel

(*above*) A male Baltimore Oriole pauses after feeding its young. Look for their pendulous sack-shaped nests along the towpath trail—typically in sycamore trees and over water.

(*opposite*) Tens of thousands of yellow iris bloom in late spring in a wetland near the Ohio & Erie Canal Towpath Trail just north of the Ira Road Trailhead. These beautiful alien flowers were probably planted by a homeowner prior to the development of the national park, and have colonized acres of the nearby wetlands.

(top)

Squirrel corn is one of the Valley spring ephemerals—short lived and fragile flowers. Found in the bottom areas of the Valley this image was taken near Brandywine creek. The simple water pattern left by a spring rain saturates the subtle colors and shapes of the squirrel corn.

(bottom)

Spring finds the Valley in a state of regeneration. Here, robber flies are mating. These insects exhibit minimal courtship behavior. The male pounces on the female much like an act of prey acquisition.

(opposite)

White narcissus bloom in early spring along Akron-Peninsula Road in Cuyahoga Valley National Park. Probably planted around a farmhouse once located nearby, the flowers have spread over the decades into the surrounding woodland.

(left)

Chippewa Creek cascades over Berea sandstone near Rte 82 on the edge of Brecksville Reservation, one of the gems in the Emerald Necklace, a popular and apt description of the 14 Cleveland Metroparks reservations covering 20,000 acres that surround the city of Cleveland.

(above)

The Green Heron's diet includes a variety of small fish, frogs and insects. Its broad diet enables it to breed on small inland ponds and marshes that won't support other herons. Here this Green Heron stands motionless waiting for a frog to emerge from the duckweed.

(above)

Dame's rocket is a beautiful but invasive alien flower that blooms along roadsides and in open woodlands in late spring throughout Cuyahoga Valley National Park. At night this flower releases an intense sweet fragrance that can be detected from a distance. This photograph was taken near Furnace Run.

(opposite)

In late-April and early May Virginia bluebells flower in large colonies along the floodplains of Cuyahoga River tributaries, especially Furnace Run and Tinker's Creek. The pinkish buds develop into blue trumpet-shaped flowers.

(top)

The delicate, pale blue, fringed flowers of Miami mist, also known as scorpionweed, appear in May in rich woods and along the Ohio & Erie Canal Towpath Trail in the Cuyahoga Valley. This plant is related to the white phacelia that blooms in large drifts in the Great Smoky Mountains.

(opposite)

Raindrops sparkle on blue cohosh leaves in the woodland understory near Furnace Run. The greenish-yellow 6-pointed flowers are replaced by bunches of deep blue berries later in the year.

(top)

Without the efforts of the beaver many of the Valley's most familiar wetland areas would not exist. Here a beaver chews on a willow shoot near its home. After eating, beavers use the peeled sticks to build a teepee-like lodge (house) on the shore and/or a dam.

(bottom)

The Rose-breasted Grosbeak is a neotropical migrant that nests in the Valley. The male Rose-breasted Grosbeak underwinging is black with a white patch and rosy wing linings that can be seen when the bird is flying overhead. The male has a lovely song described as long, liquid and robin-like.

(opposite)

The Beaver Marsh near Riverview Road, close to the southern edge of Cuyahoga Valley National Park. Beaver moved in and established a large wetland that is frequented by mink, muskrat, eastern coyote, and scores of migrating ducks, wading birds, and songbirds.

(opposite)

A burgeoning population of white-tailed deer throughout the Buckeye State has been a major factor in the dramatic decline of the large white trillium, Ohio's state wildflower. Before fading, the trillium flowers turn pink. This extensive display of trilliums was photographed along the Oxbow Trail in Cascade Metropark.

(above)

A farm lane and a historic bank barn on the old Bender Farm near Akron-Peninsula Road evoke the agricultural heritage of the Cuyahoga Valley. Recently, a Countryside Initiative has been established to help restore the rural character of the valley by re-establishing small-scale farming on several old farms in the area.

(opposite)

Wood anemone and cut-leaved toothwort announce spring's arrival in the Cuyahoga Valley. Dozens of species of spring wildflowers race to flower and set seed from late March until late May, when the emerging woodland canopy shades out the forest floor.

(above)

While not native to Ohio, the European Starling commonly nests in man-made structures such as soffits, rafters and overhangs. In the wild they prefer natural nooks and crannies like this open crevice of an aging sycamore tree near Ira Road.

(above)

Look for painted turtles in plant-filled ponds, lakes and streams. They are often seen in groups basking on logs and rocks. Sunning is important to the turtles as it regulates body temperature, aids in digestion and helps them avoid infection.

(opposite)

Several acres of yellow iris, also known as yellow flag, fill a wet depression near the Beaver Marsh along the Ohio and Erie Canal Towpath in Cuyahoga Valley National Park. The peak flowering period for this spectacular display is usually around Memorial Day in late May.

(above)

The green or purple spathes of skunk cabbage, one of the earliest spring wildflowers, appear along stream edges and other wet areas in the Cuyahoga Valley in late February and early March. The large leaves, which appear after the flowers, exude a fetid odor when crushed.

(opposite)

Leafy lanes, bridle paths, and foot trails abound in Cuyahoga Valley National Park.

(opposite)

The month of March in the Valley is incredibly quiet—winter's show is on the wane and spring has not arrived. It is still a great time to hike and notice the shape of leafless trees. The bare trees of early spring silhouetted by a setting sun of March.

(top)

In a reedy cattail nest, the mouths of Redwing Blackbird nestlings create a bouquet of red. The young birds have mistaken the movement of the photographer for their mother and open their mouths in anticipation of food.

(bottom)

The male Scarlet Tanager arrives every April to the Valley in full breeding plumage, but his shy demeanor prevents most visitors from ever noticing his courtship display. The poet James Russell Lowell might have described the male scarlet tanager best calling him the "winged flame of spring."

(top)

The cycle of life in the natural world is fragile. This Canada Goose was found dead on the side of a Cuyahoga Valley road. The pattern of dew on the Canada feathers creates a beautiful image in its death.

(bottom)

White-tailed deer cross the tracks near Red Lock. Born in late spring to mid summer, fawns will stay with their mother until the following spring. Amazingly they will not venture too far from their place of birth. If food and suitable habitat are favorable they will move less than 2 miles from that spot.

(opposite)

Deep Lock, or Lock 28, is the tallest of the 44 locks that lowered the Ohio and Erie Canal more than 300 feet from Summit Lake near Akron to Lake Erie at Cleveland. Nearby is Deep Lock Quarry, where sandstone rock was quarried to build the locks.

(above)

The tower of the Meeting House at Hale Farm & Village is reflected in the window of the log schoolhouse, built in 1816 in Summitville and moved to Hale Farm in 1965. The Greek Revival Meeting House was built in Streetsboro in 1853 and moved to Hale Farm & Village in 1970.

(above)

Canada Geese are frequent visitors to the Beaver Marsh in Cuyahoga Valley National Park, and many nest around the edges of the pond. Canada Geese are aggressive defenders of their nests, and hikers in spring on the boardwalk that crosses the beaver marsh can observe a variety of territorial behavior from these large and belligerent birds.

(top)

Canada Geese nests are very successful in the Valley but they do have their enemies—raccoons, opossums and skunks destroy eggs; foxes, crows and owls prey on goslings. This opportunistic pair built their nest some 8 feet off the ground in the safety of an old tree top, near the Boston Store.

(bottom)

The Eastern black swallowtails will search open spaces, such as meadows, gardens, banks of streams and ponds, marshes, and roadsides in search of nectar and mates. They usually flutter around, but when they are disturbed they fly straight.

(top)

Mist rises from the Cuyahoga River near Riverview Road.

(bottom)

This male Red-winged Blackbird proudly displays its bright red shoulder patches (epaulets) in attempt to lure a mate. The rich, crackly "o-ka-leeee" call nearly always accompanies the epilate display. The call of the Red-wing Blackbird means spring has arrived.

(above)

The sun rises through the branches of a willow tree at the beaver marsh near the Ira Road Trailhead. Early morning and late evening are the best times to observe the beaver, mink, mallard, wood duck, rails and other wildlife that inhabit the marsh.

(opposite)

Sunrise illuminates the Meeting House at Wheatfield, a recreation of an 1848 Ohio Western Reserve village, part of Hale Farm & Village in the southwestern part of Cuyahoga Valley National Park. The steeple, destroyed by a storm, was carefully reproduced at Hale Farm from historic images and drawings.

(top)

The 1850 Blacksmith Shop, moved to Hale farm in 1962, is used for demonstrations of nineteenth-century artisan techniques and for the fabrication and repair of many of the household items and farming implements used at Hale Farm & Village.

(bottom)

A costumed interpreter stands near one of the buildings at Hale Farm & Village, part of the Western Reserve Historical Society, the largest privately supported regional historical society in the nation.

(opposite)

The Everett Road Covered Bridge was built in 1877. It was badly damaged in the Great Flood of 1913, and washed off its supports by a storm in 1975. The Cuyahoga Valley National Park restored it in 1986. The bridge features a Smith truss, unusual in northeast Ohio.

(above)

The Yellow Creek Trading Company at 1685 Main Street in Peninsula is one of a score of retail shops, antique dealers, art galleries and restaurants that cater to visitors' needs in this picturesque village in the center of the Cuyahoga Valley.

(opposite)

The new twin concrete and steel bridges that carry Interstate 80, the Ohio Turnpike, half a mile over the Cuyahoga River valley were completed and opened in 2001 at a cost of $51 million.

(above)

Cascade Locks is a staircase of locks on the old Ohio & Erie Canal north of downtown Akron. Nearby is the restored Mustill Store, which served a canal community and included an iron foundry, a furniture plant, several gristmills, a distillery, and two rubber plants. The Cascade Locks area was placed on the National Register of Historic Places in 1992.

(above)

The fishing pier at Kendall Lake is a favorite place for young anglers and other visitors to the Cuyahoga Valley National Park.

(above)

The Cuyahoga Valley Scenic Railroad train travels south below the arches of the Brecksville/Northfield High-level Bridge over the Cuyahoga River valley in Brecksville. The photograph was taken from the Station Road Bridge, an 1881 wrought-iron truss bridge disassembled and repaired in Elmira, New York and reassembled in its original location in Brecksville for the National Park Service in 1992.

(opposite)

The RS-18 Road/Switcher was built by the Montreal Locomotive Works in 1958 for the Canadian Pacific Railroad. The Cuyahoga Valley Scenic Railroad acquired this locomotive in fall, 1998.

(above)

Boston Township Hall was originally built as Peninsula High School in 1887 of wood siding with a slate roof and bell tower. This Stick Style building was restored in 1999 and now houses Boston Township offices, the Cuyahoga Valley Historical Museum and a branch of the Peninsula Library and Historical Society.

(above)

The M.D. Garage is a restored 1940's Pure Gas Station located just east of the Cuyahoga River in the village of Boston next to the Boston Store. The garage is used to house fine art exhibits that showcase the resources of the Cuyahoga Valley.

(top)

Union officers inspect a replica of a Civil War Union cannon, on loan from Standing Rock Cemetery in Kent, Ohio, during a Civil War reenactment at Hale Farm & Village.

(bottom)

Union officers and troops prepare breakfast using authentic Civil War implements at their encampment near the Jonathan Hale House. More than 400 people participated in this reenactment, held during mid-August each year at Hale Farm & Village.

(opposite)

A line of Federal troops fires a musket volley at advancing Confederates during a battle scene reenactment staged in a pasture at Hale Farm & Village.

(top, bottom)

Confederate musicians strike up a marching tune during a Civil War reenactment at Hale Farm & Village. Below, a confederate soldier returns musket fire from Union troops during a reenacted battle scene.

(opposite)

This steam engine provides power for the sawmill at Hale Farm & Village. While its original purpose was to provide lumber for Hale Farm restoration projects, its popularity quickly grew and it soon opened for public demonstrations.

The wood-fired 1923 Frick Company steam engine, built in Waynesboro, Pennsylvania, is capable of producing pressure up to 150 lbs per square inch.

(left)

This elegant Greek Revival house was built by Jonathan Herrick in Twinsburg in 1845 from locally quarried sandstone, and was lived in continuously until 1980, when it was purchased by Western Reserve Historical Society, dismantled, and the 970 stones were catalogued and moved to Hale Farm. After reconstruction, which began in 1987, the house was re-opened to the public in 1997 as the home of the "Meredith" family, prosperous Western Reserve dairy farmers.

(above)

A white-tail buck in summer velvet rests in a valley field near the park headquarters in Jaite. The buck's antlers grow in spring with a soft covering called velvet. When antlers are "in velvet" it is the most "nutrient abundant" phase of the antlers' incredibly prolific growth cycle.

(top)

Cyclists ride across Beaver Marsh north of the Ira Road Trailhead. The boardwalk is part of the 20-mile Ohio & Erie Canal Towpath Trail that runs through the park. This trail is part of Canalway Ohio, a 110-mile National Heritage Corridor along the Ohio & Erie Canal.

(bottom)

The Canal Visitor Center is located near the northern end of the park. Permanent exhibits illustrate 12,000 years of history in the Cuyahoga Valley, including the Ohio & Erie Canal era. In the foreground is the restored Lock 38. Canal lock demonstrations are conducted by National Park staff and volunteers.

(opposite)

The observation deck along the boardwalk over the Beaver Marsh is a favorite destination for nature lovers. More than 230 species of birds have been sighted in the Cuyahoga Valley, and at the one-day International Migratory Bird Count conducted each May, 120–130 species are usually recorded.

(top)

Pottery is one of several crafts demonstrated on a seasonal basis by artisans at Hale Farm & Village.

(bottom)

This turn-of-the-century bank barn, with its gambrel roof, once stood west of Blue Hen Falls near Boston Mills Road in the Cuyahoga Valley. Like many old barns, it eventually succumbed to the ravages of time and weather, and is unfortunately no longer standing.

(above)

This 1805 log cabin, built by Jonathan Fritch in Suffield Township, was used as a hunting and fishing cabin for Goodyear Tire & Rubber Company executives and VIPs before it was moved to Hale Farm & Village in 1995 and restored. The vines near the chimney are hops, which were used for making yeast for baking…and beer! The small smokehouse was built from unused original timbers from the log cabin.

(above)

Golfers tee off on a chilly morning in late summer at Brandywine Country Club near Peninsula in the Cuyahoga Valley. This public facility has an eighteen hole Championship Course with a challenging, 575-yard, par 5 signature hole nicknamed the "Z hole", plus scenic views of the surrounding wooded hills. Near the Championship Course is a nine hole Par 3 course along the edge of the Cuyahoga river.

(opposite)

The nesting behavior of the Prothonotary Warbler is unique. They nest in holes typically abandoned by woodpeckers and nearly always over water—providing both protection and food. Most commonly seen in the bottomlands of the Valley, this nest was near Station Road bridge.

(above)

The towpath trail provides a constant show of wildflowers in the Valley. This early summer flower mix of ox-eyed daisy and tufted vetch grows near Red Lock.

(opposite)

A footbridge carries hikers and cyclists over the Cuyahoga River on the Ohio & Erie Canal Towpath Trail near the Lock 29 Trailhead in the village of Peninsula. Nearby are the sandstone foundation blocks of an aqueduct that carried the Ohio & Erie Canal over the Cuyahoga River. The exhibit in the lower right of the photograph shows the Moody and Thomas gristmill, built in 1902 on the site of an earlier mill. The Moody and Thomas gristmill burned down in 1931.

(above, opposite)

A variety of waterfowl, beaver, and other wildlife are often observed at this quiet pond near the large Beaver Marsh north of the Ira Road trailhead in the national park. Marsh marigold blooms here in early spring, followed by a spectacular display of yellow iris in late May and pickerel weed around the margin of the pond in summer.

(top)

The Frazee House was constructed in 1825 and 1826 alongside the Ohio & Erie Canal, south of the Canal Visitor Center in the northern section of the Cuyahoga Valley. The house contains exhibits on architectural styles, building construction methods during the early 1800s, and the Frazee family.

(bottom)

Less than two miles from the skyscrapers of downtown Cleveland, the Cuyahoga River emerges from its wooded corridor to flow north through the industrial Flats south of the city. The river corridor passes through Newburgh and Cuyahoga Heights before entering the park at Rockside Road in Valley View.

(above)

Shorthorn cows graze in pasture at Hale Farm & Village. The historic Milking Shorthorn breed is used mainly for its milk, but also provided meat, and was a favorite of the early pioneers.

(above)

Alexander's Mill (Wilson's Mill) was built as a flour-grinding mill in 1855. The mill was converted to turbine waterpower in the late 1800s, and used waterpower until 1970. During this period, it was converted to a feed mill. The mill is still in use today and is the only mill remaining in Cuyahoga County.

(opposite)

This photograph of Brandywine Falls, taken in late summer, required a steep climb down the cliffs below the falls to reach this vantage point. Today visitors can descend steps to a wooden boardwalk that hugs the cliffs above Brandywine Creek before reaching an observation deck very close to this viewpoint.

At 67-feet, Brandywine Falls is the tallest major waterfall in Cuyahoga Valley National Park.

(top)

The praying mantis is named for their behavior of holding up their front legs as if in prayer. They are carnivorous, feeding on a variety of insects, including moths, crickets, grasshoppers and flies. They are often protectively colored to the plants they live on. This camouflage facilitates their predatory behavior.

(bottom)

Most names given to raccoons have to do with their habits. The Latin name is *Procyon Lotor*. Lotor means washer. The name *raccoon* originated from the Algonquin word *arakun,* which means *he scratches with his hands.* Here, a curious raccoon peers out of a cavity in a maple tree.

(opposite)

This fine bank barn, with its twin ornate roof ventilators, was built more than a century ago at a farm near Akron-Peninsula Road in the southeast corner of the Cuyahoga Valley.

(above)

Tunis sheep admire the sunrise from a pasture at Hale Farm & Village. The historic Tunis breed is one of the oldest sheep breeds, dating back over 3,000 years. It is a medium-sized sheep used for producing wool and meat.

(above)

Red maple puts on a brilliant display of fall color along Brandywine Creek near Brandywine Falls. Usually the fall color peaks in the Cuyahoga Valley in mid-October. Sunny days and cool evenings encourage the chemical changes in the leaves and help to intensify the annual fall color pageant.

(top)

The Cuyahoga River cascades through a set of rapids below the Ohio Edison dam in Gorge Metropark in Summit County. The dam, built in the early 1900s, created a lake that covered most of the large waterfall for which the town of Cuyahoga Falls is named.

(bottom)

The fringed gentian is one of the Cuyahoga Valley's late summer wildflowers, displaying its deep blue color up to fall. Gentians grow in wet thickets & meadow areas and near seepage banks. While open during the day the gentian closes its petals at night, creating a well disguised perch for the katydid.

(opposite)

Brandywine Creek flows over Lower Brandywine Falls a few hundred yards downstream from the main, 67-foot Brandywine Falls. The lower falls can be reached via a scenic trail that descends from the Inn at Brandywine Falls through the woodlands along the edge of the creek.

(above)

In fall the American Robin loads up on succulent or pulpy fruits abundant in the Valley.

(opposite)

A magnificent red maple in full autumn finery towers more than a hundred feet in Tinker's Creek Gorge, a National Natural Landmark in Bedford Reservation, one of the Cleveland Metroparks in Cuyahoga County.

(top)

October in the Valley finds this male white-tailed deer in full sparring antlers. The male enters the rut to compete with other males for does. His antlers will shed by late January.

(bottom)

The milkweed plant is especially important to monarch butterflies. Caterpillars will feed solely on milkweed. In fall, when the plant goes to seed, the emerging milkweed seedpods transform this common plant into an elegant and flowing display.

(opposite)

On the far side of this autumn view of the top of Brandywine Falls can be seen the foundations of the Champion Electric Company, which produced restaurant appliances from 1920 until 1937, when the factory was destroyed by lightning.

(top)

Asian lady beetles are normally considered beneficial insects because they feed outdoors on aphids and other harmful plant pests. However, their penchant for crawling on windows, light fixtures and indoor surfaces have earned them the "pest" label.

(bottom)

Canada Geese eat roots, seeds, shoots, grain, and berries. In ponds, they eat plants off the bottom and are frequently seen with their tail and back end in the air.

(opposite)

A view looking east from Riverview Road across the open water of the Beaver Marsh north of the Ira Road Trailhead. Flocks of Canada Geese, Mallards, and Wood Ducks are common visitors to the marsh, plus occasional American Coots, Gadwall, Teal, Black Ducks and other waterfowl.

(above)

Late fall foliage radiates orange and gold along a hiking trail at Furnace Run Metropark in Richfield.

(opposite)

Fall color frames a view of Brandywine Falls, the largest waterfall in Cuyahoga Valley National Park. Several mills operated near the falls in the 1800s, including a gristmill, a sawmill, a woolen mill and a distillery that turned out 30 to 40 gallons a day of "excellent whisky."

(top)

Fall color reflects in the rapids of the Cuyahoga River at Cascade Metropark north of Akron in Summit County.

(bottom)

When insects are resting, their bodies have the same temperature as the air that surrounds them. During night this dragonfly becomes bejeweled—its wings painted in glittery dew drops.

(opposite)

Sunrise pierces the mist through the pillars and steelwork of the old Interstate 80 bridge across the Cuyahoga Valley near Boston. Explosives toppled this bridge in 2003 after construction of a new Ohio Turnpike bridge was completed.

(above)

The exquisitely colored male Wood Duck might be the Valley's most handsome waterfowl. You would think looks alone would win over a suitable mate, however, the male Wood Duck relies on other courtship behaviors as well. Wing displays, calls, and this behavior known as mutual preening which can look a lot like kissing.

(opposite)

A bird's eye view of Tinker's Creek Gorge in Bedford Reservation, one of the Cleveland Metroparks. After pouring through a stone tunnel built to carry the creek under a historic viaduct, Tinkers Creek tumbles through a rocky gorge of Berea sandstone and Bedford shale on its way to join the Cuyahoga River at Valley View.

(top)

With more than 190 species of birds recorded in the Cuyahoga Valley "birding" has become popular in the Valley. The Valley's diversified habitats of field, forest, water and edge areas provide many great opportunities for birding.

(bottom)

More states (7) claim the male Northern Cardinal as their state bird than any other bird. Its bright red color and elegant shape make it one of the most recognizable birds in any field. While not a "brag" bird by listers its flash of color on a winter day brings life to many feeders in winter.

(opposite)

A family enjoys a hike in Gorge Metropark north of Akron in Summit County. Nearby is Mary Campbell's Cave, where Mary Campbell, a young pioneer girl kidnapped in Pennsylvania in 1759 by Delaware Indians, was held captive for six years before being rescued by her family.

(opposite)

Bridal Veil Falls is a popular destination for hikers and photographers in Bedford Reservation in Cuyahoga County. Water cascades over a series of ledges of Bedford shale.

(above)

Red maples frame a section of Tinker's Creek Gorge in Bedford Reservation. The creek was named for a member of Moses Cleaveland's group who arrived to survey the area for the Connecticut Western Reserve. Tinker's Creek drops more than 200 feet in two miles.

(above)

Fall color pervades the woods along Brandywine Creek above Brandywine Falls in Cuyahoga Valley National Park.

(opposite)

Aspen, beech, maple, oak and birch are highlighted against a stormy sky in this view of the Kendall Hills along Quick Road in the eastern section of the national park. Cross country skiing and tobogganing are popular winter activities in this area.

(left)

Fishbowl Falls is one of numerous cascades along tributaries of Tinker's Creek in Bedford reservation.

(above)

A fox squirrel dines on wild berries.

(above)

The Cuyahoga Valley's most handsome duck, the male Wood Duck, stretches its wings after landing on a small pond.

(opposite)

Asters and poison ivy leaves create a fall color abstract. Poison ivy is common along roadsides, in meadows and woodland edges in the Cuyahoga Valley, and hikers learn to avoid contact with the shrub, which contains a chemical, urushiol, that causes intense irritation and a nasty skin rash when the plant is touched.

(left)

Beech and maple foliage frames a view of Blue Hen Falls, a charming waterfall along Spring Creek near the village of Boston. More resistant Berea sandstone tops the Bedford shale that forms the walls of the cascade. The shale bedrock erodes to form an undercut, with a plunge pool at the base of the falls.

(above)

In order to provide camouflage during nesting, female birds are often less colorful than their male counterparts. That does not make them any less beautiful as evidenced by this female Cardinal resting in a white pine tree.

(bottom)

Pine tree groves, some planted by the Civilian Conservation Corps in the 1930s and 1940s, are found in many areas of the national park.

(opposite)

American beech, oak and maple surround a birch tree along the rim of Tinker's Creek Gorge at Bedford Reservation.

(above)

A red fox hunts along the forest edge. The fox is extremely adept at catching mice because they can hear one squeal over 100 yards away. This fox was hunting just before sunset, but most foxes hunt at night. This photograph was made under controlled conditions.

(opposite)

A winter view of the Jonathan Hale House at Hale Farm & Village. During the past several years a $1 million restoration of the elegant three-level 1826 Federal style building has been carried out, based on meticulous 1880 records maintained by C. O. Hale.

(above)

Everett Road Bridge was washed off its abutments during a flood in 1975. When restoration began in the mid-1980s, it was discovered that very few of the salvaged original timbers were reusable. The bridge was restored with new timbers, and is a faithful reproduction of the original Smith truss bridge.

(opposite)

Tunis sheep enjoy a meal during winter at Hale Farm & Village. Presidents George Washington and Thomas Jefferson raised Tunis sheep, which originated in North Africa and today are popular in the Northeast and Midwest. They are hardy, disease resistant sheep with a lifespan of 15-20 years.

(above)

This male Northern Cardinal's feathers are fluffed up for warmth. Their beautiful red feathers work as insulation by trapping small pockets of air that are separated from the outside and warmed by the bird's body heat from within.

(opposite)

Bank barns, which are typically built on the slope of a hill or "bank," are common in the American Midwest. The entrance ramp is on the upper part of the slope behind the barn. The ornate ventilators on this handsome old bank barn helped to cool the air during summer and lower the risk of fire.

(above and opposite)

These winter scenes were photographed at the Ritchie Ledges in Virginia Kendall Park, a section of the Cuyahoga Valley National Park, after a snowstorm. The Sharon conglomerate ledges, formed more than 300 million years ago, are embedded with round quartz pebbles known as "lucky stones" or "poor man's pearls". Hemlocks and birch trees favor the cool microclimate along the Ledges.

(above)

Saw-whet owls are the smallest owl in the Cuyahoga Valley. This owl hunts almost entirely at night and rests during the day.

(opposite)

Chippewa Creek Gorge in Brecksville Reservation is a miniature wilderness of cascading rapids, giant boulders, and rocky hillsides covered with hemlock and birch trees, all within a stone's throw of the busy town of Brecksville, south of Cleveland, on the western edge of the Cuyahoga Valley.

(above)

The conspicuous ear tufts or "horns" give the Great Horned Owl its name. This one has just caught a mouse beneath the snow near Hale Farm.

(opposite)

A midwinter view of the 1852 Greek Revival Meetinghouse at Hale Farm & Village. Slated for demolition in 1969, the former Baptist Meetinghouse was acquired and moved from Streetsboro to Hale Farm in 1970.

(opposite)

Ice covers the main pond at the Beaver Marsh, as resident beaver snuggle in a well-insulated lodge. During winter, the furry rodents leave the lodge periodically to browse on the bark of willow, aspen, poplar and other trees that have been felled and stored underwater as a food cache near the lodge.

(above)

The American Robin can spend the winter in Ohio provided food is plentiful (like these crab apples) and the winter isn't too harsh. Plant foods like seeds and berries are a big part of a robin's diet. The most important plants that robins eat are in the rose family.

(left)

The wooden boardwalk over the large Beaver Marsh near the southern edge of the Cuyahoga Valley opens up the area to hikers, cyclists, and nature lovers, without impeding the activities of the industrious rodents, which can often be observed from the boardwalk in early morning and late evening during the warmer months of the year.

(above)

A Red-tailed Hawk has extremely keen eyesight and can often be seen perching in a tree at the edge of a meadow, watching for the slightest movement in the grass below.

(above)

In the fall, white-tailed deer grow long thick coats. Their winter coats are made of hollow hairs that provide insulation from the cold. Their coats and the storage of fat allow them to survive the harsh winter conditions of the Valley.

(opposite)

The Eastern or Canadian Hemlock is found in cooler areas of the Cuyahoga Valley, such as the Ritchie Ledges, shown here, as well as on the north slope of ravines like Tinker's Creek Gorge and Chippewa Gorge. The small, flat needles have two white lines and exude an odor of wintergreen oil when rubbed.

(above)

Mist softens a view of Tinker's Creek at Viaduct Park. Just downstream, Tinker's Creek flows through a tunnel in an 1865 stone viaduct before entering Tinker's Creek Gorge. Upstream are the Great Falls of Tinker's Creek and the ruins of the Holsey Gates Roller Mill.

(opposite)

Icicles line the cliffs of the Cuyahoga River Gorge in Cuyahoga Falls. Iron and other minerals leaching out of the rock have stained the ice. Upstream, on Front Street, visitors can stroll out onto a high-level observation bridge for a more distant but much safer view of the dramatic ice formations.

(above)

The handsome Red-bellied Woodpecker stores food during the winter by drilling holes into bark and hides seeds and acorns there.

(opposite)

Ice coats the trees near the Cuyahoga River south of Peninsula near Akron-Peninsula Road.

(opposite)

Spray at the base of the 60-foot Ohio Edison Dam along the Cuyahoga River in Gorge Metropark freezes on rocks and trees to create a miniature ice palace. During the warmer months, kayakers enjoy Class IV rapids for one mile through the Lower Cuyahoga River Gorge to Cascade Metropark.

(above)

A Blue Jay lights on a snow-covered pine bough. Conspicuous, and noisy, Blue Jays are capable of producing a wide variety of sounds, such as the loud *jay! jay!* call, a bell-like *tull-ull* call, as well as harsh notes and growls. They also produce a remarkable imitation of the Red-shouldered Hawk.

(above)

Many Canada Geese winter over in the Cuyahoga Valley because the river always has areas that do not freeze. Here a Canada Goose takes flight by running along the open surface of the river.

(opposite)

A late winter snowfall envelops the large pond at the Beaver Marsh. This photograph was taken before the National Park Service constructed the wooden boardwalk, now part of the Ohio & Erie Canal Towpath, in the early 1990s along the far edge of the pond.

(above)

These willows, photographed in the late 1980s at the edge of the Beaver Marsh near Riverview Road, have long since succumbed to the logging activities of the resident beaver population.

(opposite)

An oak tree with weathered roots stands guard along the east rim of the Cuyahoga Valley at Stumpy Basin near the Ohio Turnpike Bridge and the village of Boston.

(above)

This photograph is a memorial to the old barn that used to stand west of Blue Hen Falls near Boston Mills Road. "Old barns are the shrines of a good life, and ought to be remembered, " wrote Eric Sloane, the dean of Americana, in his book *An Age Of Barns*.

(opposite)

Brandywine Creek cascades over the lip of Brandywine Falls, an idyllic setting for George and Katie Hoy's Inn At Brandywine Falls behind the fence. Beautiful scenery, excellent hospitality, and fine cooking provided by the Hoys and their staff make the inn a favorite bed and breakfast destination throughout the year.

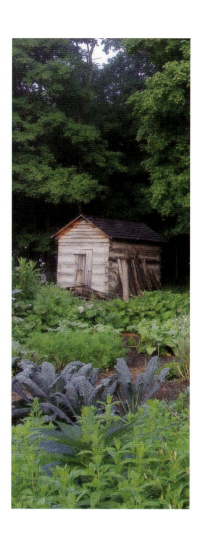

IAN ADAMS is an environmental photographer based in Cuyahoga Falls, Ohio specializing in natural, historical, and rural areas, and gardens. Since 1985, more than 4,000 of his color photographs have been published in books, magazines, calendars, posters and other publications. He has authored or co-authored ten photography books and conducted over 100 nature and garden photography workshops and seminars. His website is www.ianadamsphotography.com.

Photos: front and back jacket, pages 1, 2, 5, 7, 9, 10, 12, 13, 14, 15, 17, 18, 19, 20, 23, 24, 25, 29, 30, 31, 33, 34, 35, 36(2), 37, 38, 39, 40, 41(2), 42, 43, 44, 45, 46(2), 47, 48(2), 49, 50, 52(2), 53, 54(2), 55, 56, 59, 61, 62(2), 63, 64, 65, 67, 68, 69, 70, 71, 73, 75, 77, 78, 79, 80, 81, 83, 85, 86, 87, 88, 89, 90, 93, 94, 96, 97, 99, 100, 101, 103, 104, 105, 107, 109, 110, 112, 115, 116, 117, 119, 120, 123, 124, 125, 126, 127 and 128

JIM ROETZEL is an Ohio native who has lived in the Summit County area his entire life. Growing up near the Cuyahoga Valley National Park, he was inspired by his family's love of the outdoors and learned to see and appreciate nature through his father's eyes: "My dad had a hunter's eye and botanist's love of nature, and he most enjoyed sharing the things he loved with us." Jim's first camera was a gift from his parents, his first lessons were from his brother, and the rest of his family were his early subjects. But it was his love of being outside and exploring the Cuyahoga Valley that led Jim to focus on nature photography. An avid hiker and occasional rock climber, he believes "you have to be out in the wild almost every day to be good at this. Being outside matters most; the camera is just a way to share my walks with others." Jim has photographed all over the United States and Canada, following nature's rhythms, migrations, and seasons. His work regularly appears in many nation and local publications. When not in the field, Jim is a photography teacher at Hudson City Schools.

Photos: pages 6, 8 (2), 11, 16 (2), 21, 22, 26, 27(2), 28(2), 32(2), 33, 51, 57, 58, 60, 66(2), 70, 72, 74(2), 76(2), 81, 82, 84(2), 91, 92, 95, 98, 102, 106, 108, 111, 113, 114, 118, 121 and 122